JERUSALEM THE ETERNAL BOND

INTRODUCTION

by

Dr. Lester Eckman

President and Editor-in-chief
Judaic Research Institute
For the Publication of Works Dealing With
Judaica, Ethics and the Holocaust
Elizabeth, N.J. and Jerusalem

Jerusalem has always been engraved in the very heart of our nation. From the time it was first made holy it has been a source of values — of inner beauty, moral integrity and spiritual nobility.

Jerusalem is "the valley of vision", "a valley about which all the prophets prophesy, a valley from which all the prophets emerge".

Here is the origin of ideas and aspirations which nourish the world of all men and present the mission and challenge of mankind.

"Jerusalem will be a light to the peoples of the world, whereby they will walk". Like the image of the past is the vision for the future, since Jerusalem will become as The Land of Israel, and The Land of Israel as the whole world.

Indeed, rich and manifold are the significance and the destiny of Jerusalem. Our hope is that the legacy of our Sages of Blessed Memory presented in these pages, and which embody the essence of the eternal values of the Holy City, will serve our teachers and their pupils and will enhance and inspire the age-old saying: "Torah shall come forth from Zion and the word of God from Jerusalem".

Dr. Lester Eckman

JERUSALEM THE ETERNAL BOND

An Unbroken Link with the Jewish People

Edited by

Ruth Charif and Simcha Raz

Adviser

Dr. Lester Eckman

Published by
Judaic Research Institute
747 Livingston Rd.
Elizabeth, N.J. 07208, U.S.A.
Tel. 201-289-8029
In cooperation with
Don Publishing House

Translated into English by
Ruth P. Goldschmidt-Lehmann

Cover illustration:
View of Jerusalem.
Drawing by Daniel Vaglin, 1831

The editors thank Mr. Jacob Gellis
for putting the manuscript
of his book "Generations of Jerusalem"
at their disposal.

Design by Rochelle Don and Haim Ron
Typeset by
Monoline Press Ltd. Ramat Gan
Printed in Israel by
Yarom Press Tel Aviv

If I forget thee, O Jerusalem
Let my right hand forget her cunning.
Let my tongue
Cleave to the roof of my mouth
If I remember thee not;
If I set not Jerusalem
Above my chiefest joy.

Psalms 137:5—6

Overleaf:
Jerusalem in the 16th century.
Copper-engraving.

IERUSALEM

Contents

Dates in the
History of Jerusalem

B.C.E.

ca. 2000	In the time of Abraham, father of the Jewish and Arab peoples, the city was called "Shalem" (Salem)
ca. 1400	In the period of the Judges, held by the Jebusites, it was called "Jebus"
1000	King David captured the city and made it the capital of his kingdom
970	King Solomon built the First Temple
928	Shishak, King of Egypt, plundered the treasures of the First Temple
701	Sennacherib, King of Assyria, failed to conquer the city after besieging it
586	Nebuchadnezzar, King of Babylon, captured the city, burnt the Temple, and exiled many of its inhabitants to Babylon
539	Beginning of the Return to Zion under Zerubbabel
515	Dedication of the Second Temple
445	Rebuilding of the city begun under Nehemia and Ezra
313	City captured by Ptolemy
169	Antiochus desecrated the Second Temple
167—141	Hasmonean revolt
63	Romans captured the city
37	Herod's rule

C.E.

66—70	Revolt against the Romans
70	Roman General Titus destroyed the city and burnt the Second Temple
132—135	Jerusalem freed in the Bar-Kochba revolt
135	Emperor Hadrian destroyed Jerusalem, rebuilt it as Aelia Capitolina, and forbade Jews to enter it

362	Emperor Julian permitted Jews to settle in the city
614	Persians, with the help of the Jews, captured the city, and its government passed into the hands of the Jews for three years
629	Byzantine Emperor Heraclius captured the city from the Persians
638	Caliph Omar Ibn al-Khattab captured the city, and 70 Jewish families were permitted to settle in a quarter adjoining the Western Wall
692	Dome of the Rock built
750	Rule of the Abbassid Caliphs
1099	Crusaders captured the city and destroyed its Jewish community
1187	Saladin, Kurdish Sultan of Egypt and Syria, drove out the Crusaders
1259	Tatar invaders ransacked the city
1260	Mamluk tribes took control of the city
1267	Nahmanides and his disciples coming from Spain laid the foundations for a newly organised Jewish community
1488	Rabbi Obadiah of Bertinoro settled in the city
1517	The Turks captured the city and began four centuries of rule (except for a short Egyptian period)
1538	Sultan Suleiman built a new city wall, which surrounds the Old City to this day
1917	British army captured the city
1948	State of Israel declared
1948-49	War of Independence, and the division of Jerusalem into Israeli and Jordanian sectors
1967	Re-unification of Jerusalem after the Six-Day War

Preface

Jerusalem — the very word excites and stirs emotions, memories and glimpses of the past: The Temple. Chanting of pilgrims. Palaces and towers. Royal courts. Wars and conquests. Religious zeal. Jews wailing at the Western Wall. Aromas of incense from houses of worship. Silent tread of monks. Call of the muezzin.

Jerusalem — to be grasped with all the senses, and through one additional element: a mystery pervading this city that binds the Jewish People in an eternal bond with it.

Even when the Jews were dispersed and downtrodden among the nations and far from their homeland, they never abandoned their dream of returning to Zion and rebuilding it. And by the power of this dream, the Jewish People, a people without a country, kept its peoplehood and uniqueness alive. Moreover, Jews have always known that, while other world religions such as Christianity and Islam have several holy cities, they have only one holy city — Jerusalem — to which they turn in prayer, and only one Promised Land in which it is a religious duty for them to live.

In this book we have brought together a selection of quotations testifying to the bond between the Jews and Jerusalem. Some describe the beginnings of Jerusalem and God's choice of it as the dwelling place for the Divine Presence. Others are praises of Jerusalem or prayers for it. Some are by Jews speaking of the need to settle in Jerusalem; others, by non-Jews recognising the unique mission of the Jewish People. We have placed special emphasis on eye-witness accounts of people who actually settled in or visited Jerusalem until the end of the 19th century, before the First Aliya (the first wave of homecoming Jews from all parts of the world to Israel).

We have ended with extracts and quotations that express the hope for the redemption of Jerusalem, and the continuous expectation by the Jews of the End-of-Days, when their own restoration will be accompanied by the redemption of all mankind.

The chapters in this book are illustrated by a large number of drawings, wood-cuts and copper-engravings, selected from a great many sources, mostly ancient, the work of artists of various eras.

12

"Eternity – that is Jerusalem"

For the Jews, Jerusalem is not a city as any other. It is the Holy City, the dwelling place of the Divine Presence, the focal point of all that is Jewish.

Jerusalem is first mentioned in Genesis, where it is called "Shalem" [Salem] and its ruler is Melchizedek. That was in the 19th century B.C.E. In the 10th century it was captured by King David, who made it the capital city of the United Israelite Kingdom. It became a holy city with the building of the First Temple by David's son, Solomon.

Ever since, Jerusalem has been the political and spiritual centre of the Jewish People. Because of its holiness, all Jews — and many non-Jews — consider Jerusalem, which God chose for His "dwelling place", the centre of the world.

This chapter includes testimonies to the centrality, importance and eternity of Jerusalem as seen by the Jews.

The Blessed Holy One chooses Israel

"He standeth and shaketh the earth"
(Habakkuk 3:6) — The Blessed Holy One
considered all the nations of the world, but
found only the Jews of the generation of the
wilderness [of the Exodus from Egypt]
worthy to receive the Torah; He considered
all the mountains, and chose Sinai for the
giving of the Torah; He considered all the
cities and found only Jerusalem fit to contain
His Temple; the Blessed Holy One
considered all the countries and found only
one suitable for the People of Israel — the
Land of Israel.

(Leviticus Rabbah 13)

All hearts in the same direction

A Jew outside the Land of Israel wishing to
pray turns his heart towards the Land of
Israel; if he is in the Land, he turns his heart
towards Jerusalem; if he is in Jerusalem, he
turns his heart towards the Holy of Holies; if
he is in the Holy of Holies, he turns his heart
towards the Cover [of the Holy Ark]. Thus,
all Jews praying are directing their hearts
towards one place.

(Berakhot 30a)

Jerusalem at the World's centre

The Land of Israel is at the centre of the
world; Jerusalem is at the centre of the Land
of Israel; the Temple is at the centre of
Jerusalem; the Sanctuary is at the centre of
the Temple; the Holy Ark is at the centre of
the Sanctuary; the Foundation Stone, from
which the world was established, rests before
the Ark.

(Tanhuma, Kedoshim 10)

Opposite:
Map showing Jerusalem
at the centre of the world. 1580.

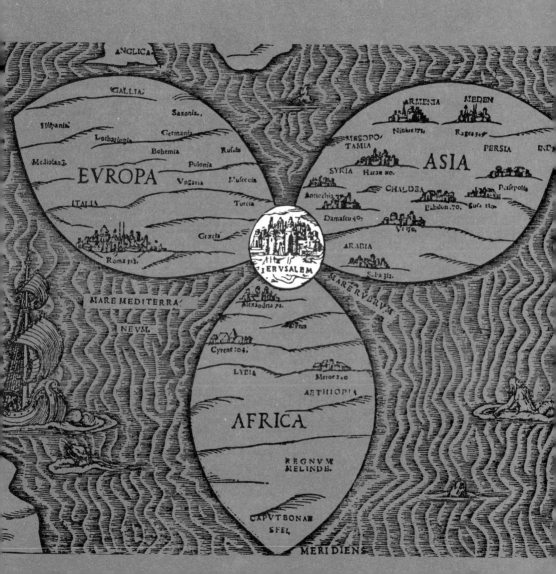

The World — like the human eye

The world is like the human eye-ball: the
white of the eye — these are the oceans
surrounding the world; the black — this is
the dry land; the pupil — this is Jerusalem,
and the lens— this is the Temple, may it be
speedily rebuilt in our days!

(Masekhet Derekh Eretz Zuta 9)

All who pray in Jerusalem

All who pray in Jerusalem pray, as it were,
before the Throne of Glory, for Jerusalem is
the gate to Heaven that is ever open to
prayer.

(Pirke de-Rabbi Eliezer 35)

Jerusalem's beauty

Ten measures of beauty descended to
the world — nine were taken by Jerusalem
and one by the rest of the world.

(Kiddushin 49 b)

Jerusalem's glory

He who has not seen Jerusalem in its glory
has never seen a beautiful city.

(Succah 51 b)

Never over-populated

"All the rivers run into the sea, yet the sea is
not full" (Ecclesiastes 1:7) — All of Israel
never come together except in Jerusalem,
and they come up several times a year on
the pilgrimage festivals — but Jerusalem is
never really filled.

(Ecclesiastes Rabbah 1)

Part of an ancient map.
West Germany.

The city that unites

"Jerusalem, that art builded as a city that is compact together" (Psalms 122:3) — the city that unites all Jews in companionship.

(Jerusalem Talmud, Hagigah 3:6)

Overleaf:
Jerusalem in the 19th century.
Lithograph.

"That ye may tell..."

Fair in situation, the joy of the whole earth;
even Mount Zion, the uttermost parts of the
north, the city of the great King. God in her
palaces hath made Himself known for a
stronghold... Walk about Zion, and go
round about her; count the towers thereof.
Mark ye well her ramparts, traverse her
palaces — that ye may tell it to the
generations following.

(Psalms 48: 3—4, 13—14)

Eternity

"...and eternity" (I Chronicles 29: 11) that is
Jerusalem.

(Berakhot 58 a)

The Tower of David.
Drawing by D. Roberts, 1838.

The Temple

The Temple — the central edifice of Jewish divine worship — was built by King Solomon in 970 B.C.E. and destroyed by Nebuchadnezzar, King of Babylon, in 586 B.C.E. It was rebuilt 70 years later by the exiles who returned to the Land of Israel with the permission of Cyrus, King of Persia, who had conquered the Babylonian Empire. Compared with the First Temple, the Second was a plain building. But during the Hasmonean period, and especially in the time of Herod, it was rebuilt on a grand and glorious scale. The Second Temple was destroyed in 70 C.E. by Roman legions led by Titus. Many of its defenders and priests threw themselves into its flames.

The Temple, which symbolised the spiritual and political independence of the Jewish People, was the central point of Jewish life. Three times a year, on the pilgrimage festivals, multitudes of Jews streamed there from all over the country and the Diaspora, to offer sacrifices and first-fruits.

Solomon's prayer
at the dedication of the Temple

What prayer and supplication soever be
made by any man of all Thy people Israel,
who shall know every man the plague of his
own heart, and spread forth his hands
towards this House; then hear Thou in
Heaven, Thy dwelling place, and forgive...
moreover concerning the stranger that is not
of Thy people Israel, when he shall come out
of a far country for Thy name's sake... when
he shall come and pray towards this House
— hear Thou in Heaven.

(I Kings 8:38—43)

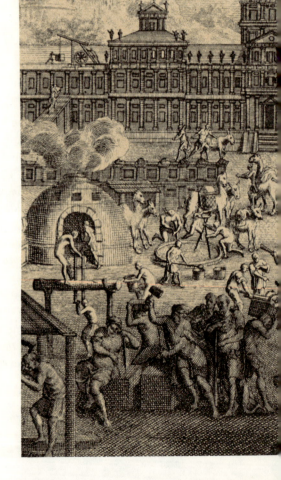

Right:
The building of the Second Temple.
17th-century copper-engraving.

23

Cyrus' Proclamation

Thus saith Cyrus King of Persia: All the kingdoms of the earth hath the Lord, the God of Heaven, given me; and He hath charged me to build Him a house in Jerusalem, which is in Judah. Whosoever there is among you of all His people — his God be with him — let him go up to Jerusalem, which is in Judah, and build the house of the Lord, the God of Israel.

(Ezra 1:2—3)

The Temple Mount's honour

One does not enter the Temple Mount [the site of the Temple] with a staff in hand, wearing shoes or a purse, or with dust on one's feet. And one does not use the Mount for a shortcut.

(Berakhot 54 a)

Beauty and splendour

We saw the city at the centre of the land of the Jews, situated on a high and exalted mountain. At its top a splendid Sanctuary has been built, and there are three walls, each more than seventy cubit high and appropriately broad and long. It is all built with an outstanding degree of splendour and beauty.

(Aristeas, 200 B.C.E.)

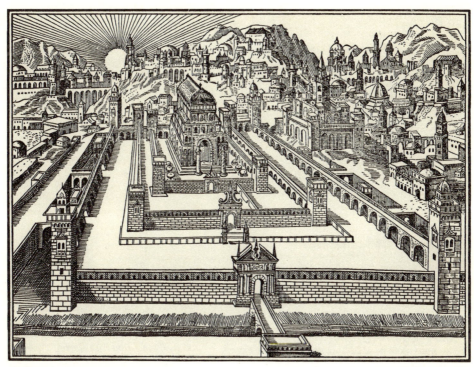

The Temple, from a Passover Haggadah
printed in Amsterdam, 1629.

Glorious building

He who has not seen the Temple in its
splendour has never seen a glorious building.

(Succah 51 b)

The Temple's appearance

The external appearance of the Sanctuary was such that it lacked nothing that would gladden the heart or please the eye. For everything was covered with heavy tablets of gold, so that at the time of sunrise its appearance was like that of a flaming torch. And when a man thought to approach the Sanctuary, he had to avert his gaze, for the sun's rays would blind him. Foreigners approaching Jerusalem had the impression of a mountain covered with snow, for the areas not covered by gold were white and shiny.

(Josephus Flavius, 1st century)

Only in Jerusalem

Since the Temple was built in Jerusalem, it was forbidden to build a House for God and to bring sacrifices anywhere else. And never may there be a Temple anywhere else except in Jerusalem, on Mount Moriah.

(Maimonides, Hilkhot Bet haBehira 1:3)

Title-page of Hebrew book, c. 1655.
At centre is drawing of the Temple, with the caption:
"And the ransomed of the Lord shall return,
and shall come unto Zion singing".

Title-page of the book
"Shaarey Dimah Viyeshuah"
[Gates of Tears and Salvation],
with picture of the Western Wall.
Printed in Jerusalem, 19th century.

Drawing from the book
"Darke Zion" [Ways to Zion],
with picture of Jerusalem
and the surrounding mountains.
Printed in 1650.

צורת הבית

The Temple Mount.
Imaginary drawing, 1750.

28

Two brothers

On the site where the Temple stood, two brothers once lived. The elder did not marry, and was all alone in the world. The younger had a wife and three children. The brothers had no material possessions except a plot of land which they had inherited from their father. They did not want to divide up the land, because they loved each other. Instead, they worked it together, and when the harvest was over they counted the sheaves and divided them equally between them, placing them in two piles, each beside his own tent.

One year, after the harvest, the elder brother lay down to sleep beside his pile. But he could not fall asleep, because the thought ran through his mind: My brother has a wife and children to care for, while I am alone in the world and I work only to fill my own belly. It isn't right that I should take an equal share with my brother. At midnight he got up, took some sheaves from his pile, stealthily went to his brother's pile and placed them there. Then he returned to his place and slept peacefully. That same night the younger brother was also unable to sleep. He thought: My brother is all alone in the world. I have sons who will look after me when I am old and unable to work. What

will my brother do in his old age? It isn't fair of me to take an equal share of the produce of our field! So before daybreak, the younger brother got up, took a few sheaves from his pile, stealthily placed them on his brother's pile, and returned to his place and slept.

In the morning, the brothers saw that their piles were as large as ever. They wondered greatly about this, but they did not say a word to each other. The same happened the next night and the morning that followed. On the third night, as the brothers were carrying sheaves to each other's piles, they met midway, recognized each other, and wept, for they realized what had been happening. They left their sheaves on the spot where they had met, and without a word returned to their respective tents. God saw what the brothers had done, and He blessed the spot where they had met. Later, Solomon King of Israel built the Temple on that very spot—the Temple from which the message of peace, love and brotherhood went out to the whole world.

(An ancient legend)

Overleaf:
Pilgrims at the Temple gates.
From title-page of a Mahzor [prayer-book for holy days]
Prague, 1834.

30

The Western Wall

The Western Wall, in the heart of the Old City of Jerusalem, is the sad remnant of the Second Temple; it is one of the Jewish People's most treasured places.

Throughout the generations — and when permitted by non-Jewish rulers — Jews have thronged to the Wall, pouring out their tears over its stones and praying for the redemption of their people and its return to the ancestral homeland. Among the Gentiles, the Wall became known as the "Wailing Wall" or "Wall of Lamentations".

During the 1948 War of Independence, the Old City was taken by the Jordanians, and the Jews were forbidden to approach the Western Wall. All attempts to persuade the Jordanians to permit Jews free access to this remnant of their Temple were in vain — in spite of the explicit undertaking of the Jordanians to do so in their armistice agreement with Israel.

After the Six-Day War of 1967, the walls dividing the city were torn down and it was reunified; and, with that reunification, the Western Wall was returned to the Jewish People.

The holiness of the Western Wall

Even though the Temple is destroyed, it [the Wall] retains its holiness... and God will never leave it.

(Midrash Exodus Rabbah 2:1)

The poor people's wall

When the Temple was being built, the work was divided among the different sectors of the population. The building of the Western Wall fell to the lot of the poor, and they worked hard to construct it, as they could not afford to hire labourers to do their work for them. When the enemy destroyed the Temple, the Angels descended from on high and, spreading their wings over the Wall, said: "This Wall, the work of the poor, shall never be destroyed".

(A Legend of the Land of Israel)

The Shechina

The Shechina [Divine Presence] will never
depart from the Western Wall, for it is said:
"Behold, he stands behind our wall" (Song
of Songs 2:9).

(Midrash Exodus Rabbah 2:2)

The Western Wall.
Drawings, 1850

Overleaf:
The Western Wall.
Drawing by Bartlett, 1842.

"Thy children shall return"

Once upon a time, the Holy Ari [Rabbi Isaac Luria, leader of the Cabbalists in the Land of Israel in the 16th century] said to his disciple Abraham Berukim: "Go up to Jerusalem and pray before the Western Wall and you will be found worthy to see the Divine Presence".
When he came before the Wall he uttered fervent prayers and supplications. After a while, he saw on the Wall a shape — that of a woman dressed in black. Shocked, he fell on his face and into a deep slumber. And then, in a dream, he saw the Divine Presence clothed in fine garb, and saying: "Be comforted, my son Abraham, for 'there is hope for thy future... and thy children shall return to their own border... I will surely have compassion'" (Jeremiah 31:17, 20).

(Folk-tale)

The Wall weeps

On the night of the Ninth of Av, the anniversary of the destruction of the Temple, in the dark of the night, there appears on the Wall a white dove — symbol of the Congregation of Israel. It spreads its wings, and keens mournfully as if joining in the people's mourning over the destruction of the Temple. And dewdrops cover the stones of the Wall. These, tradition tells us, are the tears that the Wall sheds together with the whole House of Israel.

(Ancient tale)

Prayer at the Wall

Master of the Universe. Behold, all secrets are revealed before You, and how I have taken my soul into my hand and risked my life on land and on the seas; how I have endangered my life and that of my family and brought my heart to abandon all my endeavours and all things good that I have in the Diaspora; turning my back on my children, family and friends. And You know that from the depth of my heart have I done all this for the love of the Holy Land, so that I would become worthy of settling in the Land of our Desires.

(Prayer at the Western Wall by Rabbi Samuel son of Joshua, 17th century)

Sacred once and forever

Everyone knows that there exists only one solitary wall of the Temple, and we have to lament the destruction of the Temple... Beside the Wall, the Arabs built a house of prayer and surrounded it by a wall and the

The Western Wall.
Oil painting by D. Bidas.

Western Wall is also within that wall and no one may enter. But the Jews are permitted to enter on payment of a tax... Jerusalemites pay a tax for the whole year and may enter whenever they wish, except that they must approach from outside [the Temple Mount] and not from the inside, for the original sanctity prevails forever.

(Rabbi Moses Yerushalmi, 1769)

An outcry

I do not remember how the shoes came off my feet, how I fell prostrate to the ground, how I repeatedly kissed the earth and the pavement stones beneath me, and how the tears ran from my eyes and became a mighty stream and broke like waves in my breast and the tempest raged within me. I could not, and I did not try, to control myself or the flood of my tears. I sobbed and cried like a little boy.

(Mordekhai ben Hillel Hacohen, 1896)

Pilgrims at the Western Wall. Drawing by Bidas, 1880.

The Wall of Longing

Square hewn stones, high and lofty, and worn away with age. A strange sound stirs the soul. The wail of women. The bitter weeping of men, handsome in their old age, whose beards come down over their garments. O, wall of longing, wall symbolising the profoundest grief on earth — you I touched with my burning forehead.

(Alfred Kerr, 1897)

"Since the Temple was Destroyed..."

The destruction of the Second Temple in 70 C.E. left the Jewish People in a deep shock from which it has not yet fully recovered. The destruction, the loss of national independence, and the dispersion of most of the nation throughout the world completely changed the course of Jewish history.

To keep alive the memory of the destruction, special laws and regulations were enacted, and prayers and fast-days were instituted. The main memorial observance is the Fast of the Ninth of Av, which commemorates the destruction of both the First and the Second Temple.

According to custom, the Jews mention Jerusalem both when they celebrate and when they mourn. On coming to Jerusalem for the first time, they rend their garment; and, at a wedding ceremony, the bridegroom shatters a glass underfoot. The Jewish Sages depict God Himself as mourning over the destruction of the Temple and His nation's plight.

The Elders of Jerusalem
mourning the destruction of the city.
Woodcut by Jakob Steinhardt.

No joy for God

Since the Temple was destroyed, there has been no joy for the Blessed Holy One, and it will return only when He has rebuilt Jerusalem and brought Israel back to it.

(Yalkut Shimeoni)

The Divine Presence withdraws

Until the Temple was destroyed, the Divine Presence was in its midst, as said: "The Lord is in His holy Temple" (Psalms 11:4). But when the Temple was destroyed, the Divine Presence ascended to heaven, as said: "The Lord, His throne is in heaven" (Psalms 11:4).

(Tanhuma, Exodus 10)

Mourners

Whoever mourns for Jerusalem will be privileged to see her rejoice.

(Baba Bathra 60 b)

The Redeemer is born

On the day that the Temple was destroyed, the Redeemer was born.

(Jerusalem Talmud, Berakhot 2)

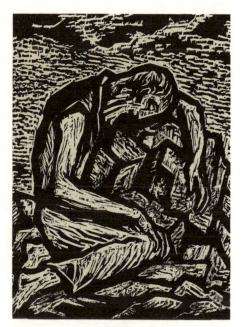

Jeremiah lamenting the destruction.
Woodcut by Jakob Steinhardt.

A dove's keening

Rabbi Eliezer entered a ruin in Jerusalem to pray, and the Prophet Elijah asked him: "What sound did you hear in that ruin?" He replied: "I heard a Heavenly Voice keening like a dove, saying, 'Woe to the children on account of whose sins I have destroyed My House, burnt My Sanctuary, and exiled them among the nations.'" Elijah said, "Upon your life and the life of your head! It speaks thus not only at this time, but three times every day!"

(Berakhot 3 a)

The pilgrimage festivals continue

"Behold, thou art fair... thine eyes are as doves" (Song of Songs 4:1) — Just as the dove never abandons its dovecot, even if its young have been taken from it, so has Israel not abolished the three pilgrimage festivals, even though the Temple is in ruins.

(Song of Songs Rabbah 4)

41

Rending one's garments

He who sees the destroyed cities of Judah says: "Thy holy cities are become a wilderness" (Isaiah 64:9) and tears his garment [as a sign of mourning]. When he sees the ruins of Jerusalem, he says: "Zion is become a wilderness, Jerusalem a desolation" (Isaiah 64:9). And when he sees the ruins of the Temple, he says: "Our holy and our beautiful House, where our fathers praised Thee, is become a pyre" (Isaiah 64:10), and rends his garments.

(Maimonides, Mishneh Torah,
Laws of Fasts 5, 16)

The mourners of Zion

After the destruction of the Second Temple, a growing number of people refused [as a sign of mourning] to eat meat or drink wine. Rabbi Judah said to them: "My sons, why do you not eat meat?" They answered him: "Should we eat meat, which was offered daily upon the altar, but now no longer?!" He said to them: "Why do you not drink wine?" They said to him: "Should we drink wine, which was poured daily upon the altar, but now no longer?!"...
He said to them: "My children, it is impossible not to mourn for the tragedy that

42

has befallen us, but to mourn excessively is also impossible, and no court should ordain anything that the public can not abide by. But our Sages have said: When a man plasters his house with plaster, he should leave a small area undone, and when a man prepares his meal, he should leave something unfinished — as a reminder of the destruction".

(Tosefta Sotah 15)

Tears of young and old

If a person would just once come from the end of the earth to pray on the Ninth of Av in the synagogue of Jerusalem, he would see there the tears being shed by young and old, by the righteous and by the simple folk, indeed by all people, and he would hear the laments, hymns and prayers — as if the Temple had just been destroyed.

(Rabbi Raphael Mordekhai Malki, 18th century)

The destruction of the First Temple. 17th-century copper-engraving.

The prisoners' song

By the rivers of Babylon, there we sat down,
yea, we wept, when we remembered Zion.
Upon the willows in the midst thereof we
hanged up our harps. For there they that led
us captive asked of us words of song, and
our tormentors asked of us mirth: 'Sing us
one of the songs of Zion'. How shall we sing
the Lord's song in a foreign land?

(Psalms 137:1–4)

"By the rivers of Babylon".
Jews mourning the destruction of Jerusalem.
Drawing by Bendman, end of 19th century.

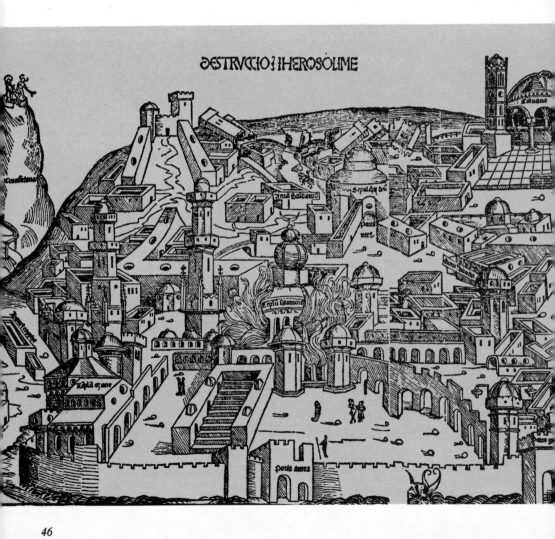

DESTRVCCIO? IHEROSOLIME

Exiled from Jerusalem

"The Lord raiseth up them that are bowed down" (Psalms 146:8). Who are they that are "bowed down"? They are the Children of Israel who are exiled from their Land. For from the day when they were exiled from Jerusalem, they have not held themselves upright.

(Midrash Shoher Tov on Psalms 146)

River of tears

Once, Rabbi Jacob David, the Amshinover Rabbi, told the Kotzker Rabbi that he had not yet seen his dead father in a vision. The Kotzker Rabbi said: "I guarantee you that you will soon see him."
While he was still in Kotzk, Rabbi Jacob saw his father and went to the Rabbi of Kotzk to tell him. The Kotzker asked him: "In what situation did you see him?" He answered: "I saw him standing by a river, leaning on his cane, as if studying the river's waters". The Kotzker said: "The river is made up of the tears of the Jews, weeping over the destruction of Jerusalem."

(Hassidic tale)

The Temple going up in flames.
Woodcut. Nurnberg, 1492 .

47

*The destruction
of the Temple.
18th-century
copper-engraving.*

The Redemption
of Jerusalem
in the Liturgy

*The Jewish Sages formulated special prayers to
commemorate Jerusalem's destruction. These prayers were
introduced into the liturgy and accepted by Jews everywhere,
and are recited up to this day. Every day the worshipper
prays: "And let our eyes behold Thy return in mercy to Zion",
and the traditional formula when comforting mourners is:
"May the Almighty comfort you among the other mourners for
Zion and Jerusalem."*

*Morning and night, on Sabbaths and holy days, in the
Grace after Meals and in the marriage service, Jews express
in their prayers their longing to see Zion comforted. They
express the hope that the People of Israel, dispersed among
the nations, will soon return to its ancestral homeland and
there renew its national and spiritual life.*

*Representative extracts from these prayers are brought in
this chapter.*

The time has come

Thou wilt arise, and have compassion upon Zion... for the appointed time is come.

(Psalms 102:14)

Comfort, O Lord...

Comfort, O Lord, the mourners of Zion, and the mourners of Jerusalem, and the city that is in mourning, laid waste, despised and desolate... for Thou, O Lord, didst consume her with fire; and with fire Thou wilt in future restore her... Blessed art Thou, O Lord, Who comfortest Zion and rebuildest Jerusalem.

(From the prayer recited on the Ninth of Av, commemorating the destruction of Jerusalem)

*The pictures
on these pages
are from the year 1637.*

The Tower of David.

The walls of Jerusalem.

Have mercy

Have mercy, O Lord our God, upon Israel
Thy people, upon the kingdom of the House
of David Thine anointed, and upon the
great and holy House that was called by
Thy name.

(From the Grace after Meals)

Rebuild it soon

And to Jerusalem, Thy city, return in mercy
and dwell therein as Thou hast spoken; and
rebuild it soon in our days as an everlasting
building... Blessed art Thou, O Lord, Who
rebuildest Jerusalem.

*(From the Amidah prayer
recited three times daily)*

Jerusalem and the Temple site.

Jerusalem.

"Lead us unto Zion"

Copper-engraving. Paris, 1840.

Bring our scattered ones among the nations
near unto Thee, and gather our dispersed
from the ends of the earth. Lead us with
exultation unto Zion Thy city, and unto
Jerusalem, the place of Thy Sanctuary, with
everlasting joy.

*(From the Amidah prayer
of the pilgrimage festivals)*

A People
Which
does not Forget

The destruction of Jerusalem, the dispersion of the Jewish People throughout the world and the suppression of their national sovereignty on the one hand; and the Jewish People's stubborn will to live, on the other — all through history these have occupied the minds of philosophers and men of conscience.

They observed this persecuted people, saw how the Jews grasped every opportunity to return to their homeland, and they understood, and occasionally even shared, the Jews' yearning to reestablish themselves in their ancestral homeland.

The quotations in this chapter are from non-Jewish sources, which speak of the special bond between the Jews and Jerusalem.

Judah's broken shell

Oh! Weep for those that wept by Babel's stream, whose shrines are desolate, whose land a dream; Weep for the harp of Judah's broken shell; Mourn—where their God hath dwelt, the godless dwell! And where shall Israel lave her bleeding feet? And when shall Zion's songs again seem sweet? And

Part of a map. 1660

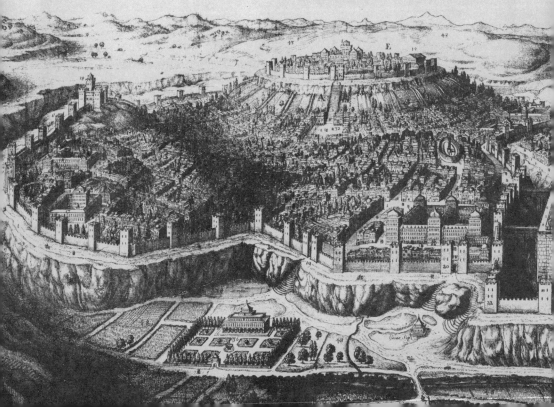

Judah's melody once more rejoice the hearts
that leaped before its heavenly voice? Tribes
of the wandering foot and the weary breast,
how shall ye flee away and be at rest! The
wild-dove hath her rest, the fox his cave,
mankind their country — Israel but grave!
(Lord Byron, 18th century)

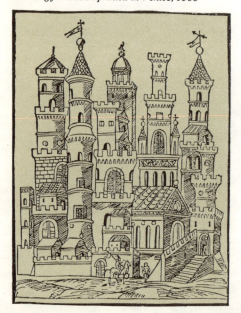

Drawing from book printed in Venice, 1500

A glorious capital

Repair the situation of the Jews, or give them a good refuge... The Jews who return to their land will have to develop arts, industry, agriculture, and commerce with Europe. Jerusalem is today a frightful hole that causes much grief to the pilgrims coming there from time to time, and it is important that she again become a glorious, populous capital, and that the waste places be transformed into habitats of civilization and culture. No longer shall these places teem with Arab bandit gangs infesting every holy place.

(Charles Josef de Linne, 1797)

Denizens of the Promised Land

It is no accident that, in spite of all the persecutions, whose like no other nation has had to endure, this nation has retained its nationhood in the course of eighteen and a half centuries... Ask yourselves if it is not of God's wise providence that the Jews should not become linked by property ownership to the various lands in which they have lived but should always remain denizens of the Promised Land, as God has commanded them forever.

(Dr. Charles Franz Zimpel, 1852)

The Wall of Jerusalem.
Copper-engraving, France, 1840.

The hope for Zion

Gaze upon the space between Mount Zion and the Sanctuary. There dwells that small people, different from all others who live in the Land. While everyone looks upon them with hatred and contempt, they quietly lower their heads without complaining of their lot... And come to the homes of these people and see how poverty-stricken and deprived they are, and how they sit and tell their children hidden mysteries in order that they may retell them to their children after them... When you see the Jewish People scattered and segregated at all corners of the world, as was prophesied by their prophets, whether their fate came to them by right or not, it is like a miraculous vision before your eyes. In order that your amazement should be complete, you should see this people in Jerusalem. There you will see these masters of this Land of Judah, the lawful owners of the Land, living as strangers and servants in their own land, and, in spite of all the pressures upon them, waiting for the Redeemer to come and redeem them. And while they are under the yoke which lies heavily upon them, they hide in the shadow of their Sanctuary, of which not one stone has remained upon another — yet they cling to their faith and do not abandon their God.

Persians, Greeks and Romans have vanished from the earth, but one small nation, more ancient still, lives on. And if there is one thing in human history which can be called a miracle — I think this is it.

(François René Chateaubriand, 1806)

The hope for return to Zion.
Drawing by A.M. Lillien.

Overleaf:
Relief from The Arch of Triumph
built in Rome in honour of Titus,
after the Romans had conquered Jerusalem
and destroyed the Second Temple.
The relief shows Jewish prisoners
carrying appurtenances taken as spoil
from the Temple.

"All we have forfeited"

You ask me what I wish, my answer is : A national existence, which we have not. You ask me what I wish, my answer is: The Land of Promise. You ask me what I wish, my answer is: The Temple, all we have forfeited, all we have yearned after, all for which we have fought, our beauteous country, our holy creed, our simple manners, and our ancient customs.

(Benjamin Disraeli, Earl of Beaconsfield, 1833)

To die where the Redemption is expected

The Jews of Jerusalem... inhabit the quarter between Mount Zion and Mount Moriah, where their synagogues are situated... They come from different and distant countries and are attracted to Jerusalem by their desire of inhabiting the Valley of Jehosaphat and to die on the very place where the Redemption is to be expected... They suffer and pray, their regard turned to that mountain of Moriah where once rose the Temple of Lebanon, and which they dare not approach; They shed tears on the misfortunes of Zion and their dispersion over the world.

(Karl Marx, 1854)

A vital necessity

We are living in an age in which each and every nation has decided to ask for the return of its own country, home, language, and sanctuary. For too long have the Children of Israel been deprived of all this... We are not prepared to remain a sect; we wish to be a people. More than that: a nation. A spiritual homeland no longer suffices us. A real, earthly homeland is becoming a vital necessity for us, and I shall go to demand it, and to obtain our legitimate birth certificate... Next year in Jerusalem!

(Alexandre Dumas, fils, from his play, La Femme de Claude, 1873)

A people which mourns 2000 years

It happened once that Napoleon was passing by a synagogue on the Ninth of Av, at the time when the worshippers were sitting on the floor reciting elegies and weeping. "Why are they weeping?" he asked. They explained to him that they were weeping for their country which was destroyed nearly 2000 years ago.

The explanation made a profound impression on the French emperor, who said: "A people that mourns and weeps for the loss of its homeland 2000 years and does not forget — such a people will never be destroyed. Such a people can rest assured that its homeland will be returned to it."

(Folk-tale)

Overleaf:
Jews mourning in Synagogue
on the Ninth of Av,
/the national day of mourning
for the destruction of the Temple/.
Woodcut. Amsterdam, 1723.

Next Year in Jerusalem

*"My heart is in the east, and I am in the uttermost west",
wrote the twelfth-century Spanish-Jewish poet Judah Ha-Levi.
He was expressing the feelings of his brethren who, though
scattered throughout the Diaspora, had their hearts focussed
on their one and only homeland — Zion.*

*Just as there were always some Jews living in the Land of
Israel, so were there always Jews coming home from exile.
The profound yearning for Zion, the urge to return and
reestablish the Jewish state, and the faith that the vision of the
Prophets would be fulfilled — all this sustained the spirit of the
Jews in all the countries of their dispersion. Jewish religious
writings throughout history have stressed the religious
obligation to come home to the Land of Israel, and indeed
individuals and groups came in the most difficult and
dangerous of times to resettle it.*

*The resettling of Jerusalem has always symbolized the
revival of the Land of Israel. On festive occasions, and
especially on the eve of Pesach and on Yom Kippur,
Jews pray: "Next Year in Jerusalem!"*

Going to Jerusalem

Everyone goes to Jerusalem: a man may compel his family to settle with him in Jerusalem; even a woman may compel her husband to go there with her to live.

(Rashi, Ketubot 110 b)

The longing

Jerusalem will be rebuilt when the Jews' yearning for it will be complete, to the degree that they will love its very stones and soil.

(Judah Ha-Levi, 12th century)

Anticipating the Messiah

Those who deceive themselves and say that they will remain where they are until the Messiah comes to the West, and will only then set out themselves for Jerusalem Indeed they sin and lead others to sin, for there is no specific time for the coming of the Messiah, and one cannot be sure and say that it is near or far off.

(Maimonides, On Forced Conversions, 1164)

The oath

We two, Rabbi Hiskiyah and I, swore to go up to the Land of Israel, and we fixed the time of departure for two years after the oath. When the time came, we sold all our possessions and household goods and bought goods and food for the journey... and we left behind in Cordova our wives, sons and daughters and all that we had.
And this was our oath: "We have vowed unto the God of Jacob to go up to the Land of Israel and live in or near Jerusalem, for there it is fitting to observe the religious commandments and accept the Kingdom of Heaven and serve, for there is the House of our God and the gate to Heaven" — and we swore unto each other on the Scroll of the Law. And if, Heaven forbid, we do not both find a livelihood, one will devote specific times to study, and the other will try... to provide for him who has devoted his time to the study of the Torah and for his household... and everything that we earn we shall share between us...

(Rabbi Jacob Skili, 14th century)

Let us go up

A call went out from God... The masses of the people of the God of Abraham gathered from the east and from the west, some by ship over the high seas, some across mountainous wastes, to go up to the city surrounded by mountains and crawl in its dust... Come let us go up to the mountain of the Lord, with our sons and daughters, so that there we may resume our encounter with the Torah and with our mission.

(Rabbi Hayyim ben Attar, 1742)

Overleaf:
The Messiah reaching Jerusalem.
From a Passover Haggadah, Venice, 1665.

The Temple. Drawing from an old Haggadah /text read on eve of Passover/

ירושלם

Remembering Jerusalem

Every Jew has to promise himself to go and live in the Land of Israel and to yearn for the privilege of praying there before God's Sanctuary; and even though it is destroyed, the Divine Presence has not left it. So hear me, brothers and friends, remember Jerusalem... and do not, Heaven forbid, think of settling outside the Land.

It seems to us that as soon as we enjoy some tranquillity outside the Land of Israel, it is as though we have found another Land of Israel and another Jerusalem, and that is why all these evils have come upon us.

(Rabbi Jacob Emden, 1745)

Right:
King David and the Children of Israel dancing before the gates of Jerusalem. 17th-century copper engraving.

A joyous face

We have seen with our own eyes that one who takes up residence in the Land of Israel as a burden, with downcast spirit—his life here is all pain, and he wonders why he ever forsook the pleasures of life in the Diaspora... The Holy Land, too, withholds itself from him. Whereas one who takes up residence in Jerusalem joyously and lovingly—the Holy Land also absorbs him and receives him gladly, so that living in the Land of Israel seems to him like life in the Garden of Eden... even if he is living in the meanest of places and even if in the Diaspora he had houses filled with all the good things.

(Rabbi Isaac Farhi, 1840)

Taking possession

With every parcel of land that we purchase, we are observing the commandment to take possession of the Land, and this is greater then all the Torah's commandments. Of course, in merely purchasing land we are not yet fully observing this commandment, which includes living in the land of our ancestors and in Jerusalem our holy city and making it a beautiful land by planting and sowing in it.

(Rabbi Samuel Mohilever, 1890)

Settling the Land

Awake, awake, be of good courage, children of Zion and Jerusalem! For God is with us. And what does God ask of us but a pure heart and a soul longing for our holy soil? Awake, dear brethren! Let us get to working. Let us cease waiting for the End-of-Days—that is, for our brethren in the Diaspora to buy us fields and vineyards and to arrange our lives for us... It is you whom God has chosen to clear the way, to pave the road—the road to the settlement of the Holy Land.

(Joel Moses Solomon, 1877)

The Redeemer will come

The Tzechinover Rabbi Abraham was wont every year to come to synagogue on the Ninth of Av with a new copy of the Elegies [lamenting the destruction] in his hands. He used to recite the Elegies, and when he had finished he would leave the book in the box under the lectern.
When asked the reason, he used to say: "I am sure that next year the Redeemer will come to redeem us from exile and restore us to Jerusalem—so we will no longer need to recite the Elegies."

(Hassidic tale)

The wedding in Jerusalem

In betrothal contracts written in the home of Rabbi Levi Isaac of Berditchev, it was stipulated: "The wedding will, God willing, take place in the Holy City of Jerusalem. But if, Heaven forbid, because of our sins, the Messiah will not have come by then, the wedding will take place in Berditchev".

(Jewish folk-tale)

The Messiah has not yet come?

On the Ninth of Av [the national day of mourning for the destruction of the Temple], the Rabbi of Tchortkov, Rabbi David Moses would sit with his head between his knees, streams of tears flowing around him. Now and then he would raise his head and ask: "Not yet? The Messiah still has not come?!"

(Hassidic tale)

A drawing from a Passover Haggadah, *with the blessing "Leshana Habaah Biyerushalaim" [Next Year in Jerusalem]. Printed c. 1709.*

לְשָׁנָה הַבָּאָה בִּירוּשָׁלַיִם.

"Within
thy Gates..."

Immigrants, pilgrims and tourists of various nations have come to Jerusalem and described the experience of their meeting with the city.

Many Jews coming back to Jerusalem to settle there, or as pilgrims and tourists, have described what they felt on arriving at the city of their hopes. A Jew's first encounter with the Holy City gives rise to a storm of emotions: joy at the privilege, and sorrow at the sight of the destruction. These first impressions are recorded mainly in letters sent back to foreign lands, reporting simply and plainly on what is happening in the city.

For this chapter we have selected a few out of the vast collection of them. One thought runs through them all: Jerusalem and the Jewish People are inseparable.

The pierced stone

At the side of the Sanctuary there is a pierced stone. Jews visit there once a year, pour oil over it, lament and weep over it, and tear their garments in token of mourning. Then they return home.

(Itinerarium Burdigalense —
The Pilgrim of Bordeaux, 333)

A wretched people

Up to this day it is forbidden for the treacherous citizens to enter Jerusalem... they may enter only to lament there, and they have to pay for the right to weep over the ruins of their state; not even once are they permitted to weep free of charge. And on the anniversary of the day when the city fell and was destroyed by the Romans, there are crowds who mourn, old women and old men dressed in tatters and rags, and from the top of the Mount of Olives this wretched throng laments over the destruction of its Sanctuary. Still their eyes flow with tears, still their hands tremble and their hair is dishevelled, but already the guard demands his pay for the right to weep.

(Jerome, 392)

Jerusalem with Solomon's Temple at its centre.

The ruins

On that selfsame area upon which the Temple once stood in its glory, and near to the Eastern Wall, the Arabs now visit a house of prayer constructed of beams and boards which they have erected on the ruins...

(Arculfus, c. 670)

Negotiations with Omar

And all the Moslems of the city [Jerusalem] and the surrounding settlements came, accompanied by a group of Jews. The Caliph Omar commanded them to clean up the Temple site. He asked the Jewish elders about the *Sahra*—that is, the Stone of the Foundation—and one of the Jewish wise men showed him where it should be, and they removed the rubble and found the Stone... The Jews then asked Omar: "How many Jews will be permitted to live in the city?" He replied: "What do your enemies [the Christians] say?" The Christian Patriarch said: "Fifty Jewish families." The Jews said: "Not fewer than two hundred families." And they bargained, till Omar decided on seventy families, and the Jews agreed. Then Omar

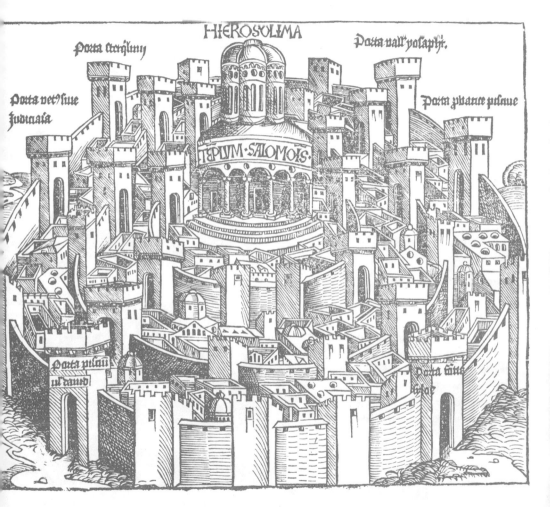

HIEROSOLIMA

Porta ctergliny

Porta vall' yosapht.

Porta vet'sue
Judicaia

Porta phante pisaue

TEPLUM SALOMOIS

Porta pilati
ul dauid

Porta fonte
Siloe

asked: "Where do you wish to live?" The Jews asked to live in the southern part of the city—that is, in the area of the Jews' Market, for they wished to live near the site of the Temple and its gates.

*(From a document found
in the Cairo Genizah, 9th century)*

500 years of restrictions

For 500 years Jews could not enter Jerusalem without risking their lives... However, when the Ishmaelite Kingdom was founded, they were permitted to settle in the city... but later the Ishmaelites wanted to expel them altogether.

(Salman son of Yeruham, 981)

Evildoers have come

Hail to our brothers and fellow faithful, greetings from the Faithful City and from the president of the *Yeshivah* in Zion. We wretched few inform you... that evildoers have entered our God's Sanctuary... intruders have come and defiled it... and we can find no comfort except in prostrating ourselves and begging for mercy and forgiveness, entreating Him to return to Jerusalem in mercy and purify His

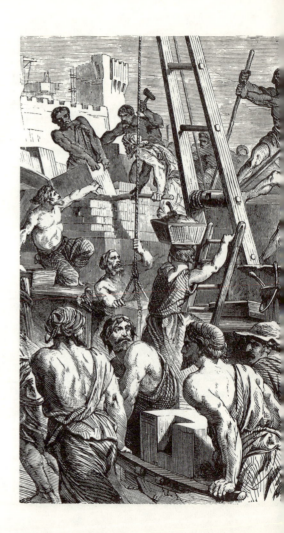

Sanctuary and raise it from its dust...
We, your poor brothers, who pray for you in
the Holy City of the living God,... have
undertaken to look to the needs of the city,
to clean it and repair its walls. Had we not
done so, we could not have lived with them...
or encompassed the gates on the Mount of
Olives or raised our voice in prayer. And all
this only at the cost of much bribery,... and
at the present time we can depend on
nothing except the mercies of Heaven and
our brethren of the House of Israel.

*(Letter from the leaders of the Jewish community
in Jerusalem to the Diaspora, 977)*

Jerusalem Yearns

...And let our brethren know that Jerusalem
is yet desolate and yearning for its dispersed
sons. How long will you neglect the Land of
the Almighty, while the Chosen Land
remains in the hands of your enemies? And
Jerusalem is today the refuge of all who flee,
a comfort for all mourners, and a place of

*The building of the Temple.
19th-century drawing.*

rest for the poor and deprived. And in its
midst God's servants congregate from afar...
and among them are women lamenting in
the language of Ishmael. And in the months
of Tammuz and Av [when the Destruction
took place] the mourning is great, men fast
and afflict themselves by wearing sackcloth,
and going up to the Mount of Olives.

(Sahal son of Mazliah, 1010)

Dyers

There is a dyeing plant in Jerusalem which
the Jews rent from the king each year,
thereby also acquiring the exclusive right to
be the city's dyers. They live at the edge of
the city, below the Tower of David. Omar
built a large and beautiful dome on the site
of the Temple. Nearby is the Western Wall,
to whose court all the Jews come. The
Mourners of Zion and the Mourners of
Jerusalem eat no meat, drink no wine, wear
black clothes, live in caves or hidden hovels,
and fast every day of their lives.

(Rabbi Benjamin of Tudela, 1165)

The three hundred rabbis

In the year 1211 God stirred the rabbis of
France and England to come to Jerusalem.

There were more than three hundred of them, and the king paid them great honour and built them synagogues and study-houses there.

(Rabbi Solomon ibn Verga, 16th century)

"Now I can die"

And I turned towards God's mountain and the city which God has chosen... and when I came unto her borders, I said: "How goodly are thy tents, Mount Zion, and thy dwelling-places," and "Now I can die, since I have seen thy face" (Genesis 46:30).
And I saw one of the city's dwellers and asked him: "When did the Jews come to this city?" And he said to me: "When the Ishmaelites captured it." I said: "And why was the city not inhabited when it was in the hands of the non-Jews?" He replied: "Because they said we had murdered their god, and disgraced them, and had they found us alive, they would have swallowed us up alive."
And from there I travelled to Jerusalem, and messengers of the Lord met me: these are the pious of the Most High who have come from France to dwell in Zion under the leadership of the great and pious Rabbi Joseph the son of Rabbi Barukh, and his brother, the Sage Rabbi Meir. And we

tarried in the city for a month, and every day visited the graves and other notable sites, and wept over Zion and the graves of the righteous.

(Rabbi Judah Al-Harizi, 1218)

Travellers to Jerusalem

I am writing you this letter from the Holy City of Jerusalem... what can I tell you about the country? Great is the misery, and great the devastation, and, in brief, the more sacred the place, the greater the desolation; Jerusalem is more devastated than the rest of the country, and Judah more than Galilee; but in spite of its desolation the Land is good.
There are about 2,000 inhabitants, including about 300 Christians, refugees who escaped the sword of the Sultan; but there are no Jews. For after the arrival of the Tatars the Jews fled and some were killed by the sword. There are now only two brothers, dyers, who buy their dyes from the government. At their place, a quorum of worshippers meets on the Sabbath. And we encouraged them and found a ruined house, built on pillars and with a beautiful dome, and made it into a synagogue; for the town has no ruler and whoever wishes to take a ruin, can do so.

Jerusalem and the Holy Places.
Drawing, c. 1850.

And we volunteered to restore the building, and they have already begun and sent to the city of Nablus for the Scrolls of the Law which had been in Jerusalem, but were taken away when the Tatars came. And now they have established a synagogue, where they will pray. For people regularly come to Jerusalem, men and women, from Damascus and from Aleppo, and from all parts of the country, to see the Temple and weep over it.

And may He Who has deemed us worthy to see Jerusalem in her ruins grant us to see her rebuilt and restored and the honour of the Divine Presence returned. And may you, my son, your brothers and your father's house all be worthy to witness the good of Jerusalem and the comfort of Zion.

(Nahmanides' letter to his son, 1267)

The true science

In Jerusalem there have gathered Jewish families from all parts of the world, especially France. Among the men of Jerusalem are many handicraftsmen, especially dyers, tailors, and cobblers. Others flourish in business. Some engage in

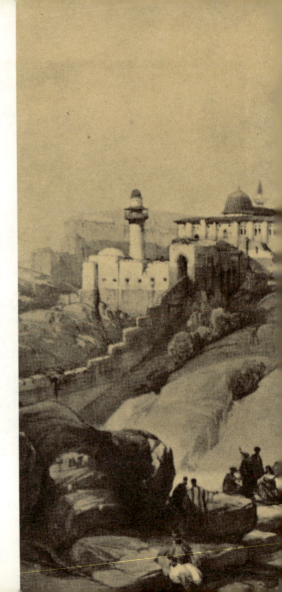

The Temple Mount and the Dome of the Rock. Drawing by D. Roberts, 1842.

the sciences. But most of the scholars are engaged day and night in the study of the sacred lore, the true science, Cabbala, and they are supported from the communal coffers. There are also master scribes in Jerusalem.

(Isaac Helo, 1335)

The Redemption

Some of the miracles of Jerusalem still exist; for instance, a person can never say: "There is no room for me." The people of Jerusalem filled the synagogue in Jerusalem all year round. And when it was filled to overflowing on the Feast of Pentecost — which was celebrated by more than 300 people — all could enter and sit down comfortably — for its holiness remained. And this is one of the signs of the Third Redemption.

(Rabbi Simeon son of Zemah Duran, c. 1420)

Mourning

I arrived in Jerusalem in June, 1481. When I beheld the city's ruins, I tore a long rent in my garment and said a prayer... All the Jews of the city go to Mount Zion every year on the Ninth of Av to mourn and weep. From there they go down to the Vale of Jehoshaphat and ascend the Mount of Olives, from which it is possible to see the

The Messiah arriving in Jerusalem. Drawing, beginning of 16th century.

entire Temple area, and they mourn over the destruction of the Temple.

(Rabbi Meshullam of Volterra, 1481)

There is hope

When we arrived in Jerusalem, we were unable to decide whether to thank God for having arrived whole, or whether to weep over our sins, and our spirit failed us and we could not bring ourselves to rejoice. In Jerusalem there is a poor and wretched remainder of people sheltering themselves in God's Name and praying morning and evening. There is no frivolity or prostitution here, and there is hope of Redemption, may it come soon!

I adjure you to copy out the contents of this letter and transmit it to the communities in your vicinity, and bid them to convey it from community to community, so that they shall all pray to God to rebuild His city and restore its glory along with that of His people.

(Rabbi Isaac Latif, 1485)

Rending the garments

As soon as the famous city of our delight came into view, we rent our garments — as was our duty — and as we approached still nearer, there was revealed before us our glorious and destroyed Sanctuary, and again we rent our garments... No Jew may enter the Sanctuary, although the Ishmaelites have often tried to persuade Jews to enter there to do carpentry and all other sorts of work, but the Jews refuse to enter.

(Rabbi Obadiah of Bertinoro, 1488)

The Jews refuse to leave

The Christians and Jews of Jerusalem lack all resources and find themselves in dire straits. There are but few Christians, but there are many Jews... A Jew whose house collapses is not permitted to build a new one in its place, but must again buy the plot from its owner at a high price. Christians and Jews go about Jerusalem dressed as would beggars in our country; they are not permitted to wear good coats. But in spite of all the troubles and the oppression that they suffer at the hands of the non-Jews, the Jews refuse to leave the place.

(Martin Kabatnik, 1491)

My heart

My heart yearned to go to the Holy City of Jerusalem. And I went by sea and arrived in Jaffa. From there I first proceeded to Hebron, from there to the Kidron Valley, and from there I went up to Mount Zion, the place of the Sanctuary. And I went about the city, and my heart burned within me for the city of my forefathers and its ruins.

(Rabbi Zechariah Al-Sahari, 1567)

Zion's comfort

I have already reported to you how good the Almighty has been to me; how I left Safad and entered Jerusalem which lacks nothing... My wife and I thank God that we are worthy to serve Him. May it be God's will that we shall be found worthy to live and witness — together with all of Israel — the comfort of Zion.

(Rabbi Simeon Bak, 1584)

Paying taxes

In Jerusalem there are a few Jewish families, who are permitted to live there provided they pay the annual taxes and do not contravene the instructions of the *Kadi* [Moslem judge] of the city.

(Nicolas Bénard, 1617)

Crowded

Jerusalem, though in ruins, is yet the joy of the whole earth, and is tranquil, and possesses good and choice wine... Glory to God—Jerusalem has become crowded, for the community is growing from day to day, and large buildings are being built, all of which we consider to be a sign of the approaching Redemption, may it come speedily!

(Rabbi Isaiah ha-Levy Hurwitz, 17th century)

Aid from the Diaspora

The situation of the Jews of Jerusalem of late was such that they were unable to subsist without the aid of their brethren in the Diaspora, because the place does not offer the possibility of any work at all, or offers only very little. But their love for the place prompts them to remain there, albeit in great poverty and want. And their brethren in the Diaspora, living among the nations, displayed their desire to support them so

Opposite:
Embroidery. 1928.
(From the S. Pappenheim Collection).

כותל מערבי

that the place should not remain without at least a few members of their nation to watch over it as though it were their possession, and to demonstrate their hope until the full resurrection shall come to pass.

(Henry Jessie, 1658)

The gates to Paradise

On the Eve of the Day of Atonement we went to the synagogue in Jerusalem and there was a great illumination at the time of the Kol Nidrei prayer. When I opened the Holy Ark, I felt as though I was opening the gates to Paradise... and everyone was praying and weeping bitterly to God for the rebuilding of the Temple.

(Rabbi Hayyim ben Attar, 1746)

Twenty thousand Jews

The populace of Jerusalem includes about twenty thousand Jews. Most of them are paupers. They have no source of livelihood, except what they are able to obtain from pilgrims of their own nation who travel great distances, coming from everywhere, to express their affection for their ancestors' habitation.

(Friedrich Hasselkvist, 1751)

Jerusalem and its surroundings. Part of a map, 1875.

Synagogues and yeshivot

Jerusalem has more than three thousand Jewish families—native-born and those who have come from all parts of the world. They have five synagogues, three for the native-born Jews and those who have come from Muslim lands and are known as Sephardim, and two for the European Jews who are known as Ashkenazim. They have five study-houses called *yeshivot* in Hebrew. The Jews speak the following languages: Spanish, Arabic, German, Italian, and English. When the Sephardim and Ashkenazim meet, they converse in Hebrew.

(Rabbi David Debeit Hillel, 1824)

Desire of my youth

Greetings, beautiful and holy homeland! From faraway places have I come to you. For years have I yearned to walk on your soil; for years have I longed for you and suffered for you in the Mountains of Carpathia and Galicia, in the steppes and plains of Hungary, and in the northern and eastern states of America.
You were the desire of my youth, and the dream of my adolescence, and now that I have reached the threshold of my old age, the hope still burns in my heart to grasp you, to know that in truth you are the inheritance of your sons and daughters... they will re-establish in your midst their national home.

(Simon Berman, 1870)

Overleaf:
Jerusalem. French copper engraving, c. 1840.

Jerusalem and its Surroundings. Map, 1615.

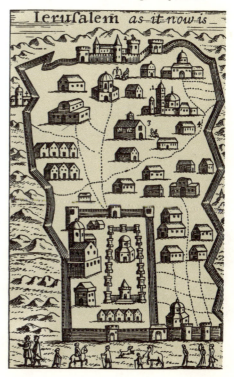

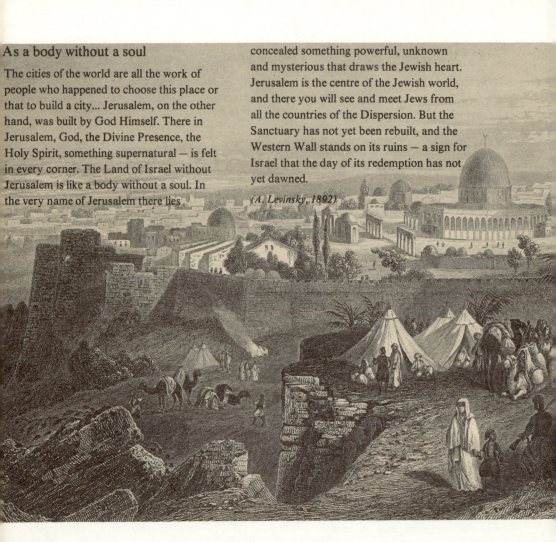

As a body without a soul

The cities of the world are all the work of people who happened to choose this place or that to build a city... Jerusalem, on the other hand, was built by God Himself. There in Jerusalem, God, the Divine Presence, the Holy Spirit, something supernatural — is felt in every corner. The Land of Israel without Jerusalem is like a body without a soul. In the very name of Jerusalem there lies concealed something powerful, unknown and mysterious that draws the Jewish heart. Jerusalem is the centre of the Jewish world, and there you will see and meet Jews from all the countries of the Dispersion. But the Sanctuary has not yet been rebuilt, and the Western Wall stands on its ruins — a sign for Israel that the day of its redemption has not yet dawned.

(A. Levinsky, 1892)

In Time
to Come

The Jewish Prophets' words of comfort were a balm to the generation that witnessed the destruction, and to all the generations that followed. Particularly during periods of persecution the Jews in the Dispersion clung to the vision of the Jerusalem-to-Be, a city in all its glory. Indeed, faithful Jews await and pray daily for the Final Redemption and God's return to Zion.

That hope is not just a fleeting longing of the Jewish People to be independent in its own homeland. It is a hope for the End-of-Days promised by Jerusalem's Prophets as a symbol of everlasting peace for all mankind.

"Comfort ye, My people"

Comfort ye, comfort ye, My people, saith
your God. Bid Jerusalem take heart, and
proclaim unto her, that her time of service is
accomplished, that her guilt is paid off; that
she hath received of the Lord's hand double
for all her sins... O thou that telleth good
tidings to Zion, get thee up unto the high
mountain; O thou that telleth good tidings to
Jerusalem, lift up thy voice with strength; lift
it up, be not afraid; say unto the cities of
Judah: 'Behold your God'.

(Isaiah 40:1–2, 9)

Drawing of the Temple.
From Hebrew book printed in 1551.

The Messiah at the gates of Jerusalem.
From a Passover Haggadah. *Mantua, 1561.*

"Boys and girls playing"

Thus saith the Lord: I return unto Zion and
will dwell in the midst of Jerusalem; and
Jerusalem shall be called the City of Truth;
and the Mountain of the Lord of Hosts —
the Holy Mountain. ...there shall yet old men
and old women sit in the broad places of
Jerusalem, every man with his staff in his
hand for very age. And the broad places of
the city shall be full of boys and girls playing
in the broad places thereof.

(Zechariah 8:3–5)

Where the Messiah will dwell

They said to the Messiah: "Where do you
wish to dwell?" "What a question to ask!
:'On Zion, My Holy Mountain' " (Psalms
2:6).

(Yalkut Shimeoni, Psalms, 620)

"They all are gathered"

Arise, shine, for thy light is come, and the
glory of the Lord is risen upon thee... Lift up
thine eyes round about, and see: they all are
gathered together, and come to thee, thy
sons come from far, and thy daughters are
borne on the side... And the sons of them
that afflicted thee shall come bending unto
thee, and all that despised thee shall bow
down at the soles of thy feet; and they shall
call thee the city of the Lord, the Zion of the
Holy One of Israel.

(Isaiah 60: 1, 4, 14)

The way of Redemption

Rabbi Hiyyah Rabba and Rabbi Simeon ben Halafta were walking along one morning when dawn broke. Rabbi Hiyyah said to Rabbi Simeon: "That is how the Redemption of Israel will come about, at first little by little, and then the more light there is, the more it will increase and spread forth".

(Jerusalem Talmud, Berakhot 1)

"For Zion's sake"

For Zion's sake I will not hold My peace, and for Jerusalem's sake I will not rest, until her triumph goes forth as brightness, and her salvation as a torch that burneth... I have set watchmen upon thy walls, O Jerusalem, they shall never hold their peace day or night.

(Isaiah 62: 1, 6—7)

Ingathering of the exiles

Jerusalem will be rebuilt only when the exiles have been gathered in. So if someone tells you that all the exiles have returned, but Jerusalem has not yet been built, do not believe him, for it says (Psalms 147: 2): "The Lord doth build up Jerusalem" and only after that comes: "He gathereth together the dispersed of Israel".

(Tanhuma, 58)

A light unto the nations

In time to come Jerusalem will become as a torch unto the nations of the world, and they will walk in its light.

(Pesikta Rabbati)

Part of a map of Jerusalem. 1483.

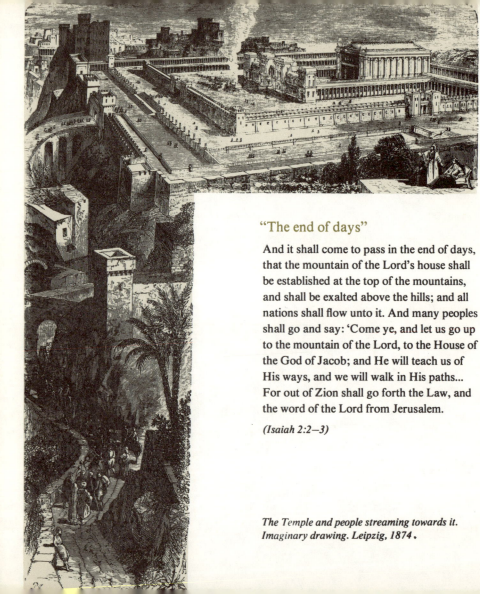

"The end of days"

And it shall come to pass in the end of days, that the mountain of the Lord's house shall be established at the top of the mountains, and shall be exalted above the hills; and all nations shall flow unto it. And many peoples shall go and say: 'Come ye, and let us go up to the mountain of the Lord, to the House of the God of Jacob; and He will teach us of His ways, and we will walk in His paths... For out of Zion shall go forth the Law, and the word of the Lord from Jerusalem.

(Isaiah 2:2—3)

The Temple and people streaming towards it. Imaginary drawing. Leipzig, 1874.

The southern wall of Jerusalem.
Woodcut, 1881.

Sources

Al-Harizi, Judah. c. 1170—1235. Poet, born in Spain. Extract from his book *Tahkemoni.*

Al-Sahari, Zechariah. Rabbi, born in Yemen. Visited Jerusalem in 1568.

Arculfus. French Bishop. Visited the Land of Israel c. 697. Extract from his book on the Land of Israel.

Aristeas. Jew connected with the Egyptian Court. Visited the Land of Israel in 200 B.C.E.

Bak, Simeon. Came to the Land of Israel from Italy in 1582. Extract from letter which he sent to his relatives in Italy in 1584.

Barnett, Zerach. 1843—1935. Active in settlement movements, born in Kovna, Russia. Founder of a Yeshiva near Jaffa. Came to Israel in 1871. Extract from his essays.

Ben Attar, Hayyim. 1696—1743. Rabbi, Cabbalist, commentator and legalist, born in Morocco. Came to the Land of Israel in 1741. Extract from letter which he sent from Jerusalem to Italy in 1742.

Ben Hillel Hacohen, Mordekhai. 1856—1936. Publicist, active in the early Russian Zionist movement "Hovivey Zion" (Lovers of Zion). Extract from his book *From Evening to Evening.*

Bénard, Nicolas. From Paris. Visited the Land of Israel in 1617.

Berman, Simeon. 1818—1884. Born in Cracow. Extract from his Yiddish book *Mas'ot Shim'on* (Travels of Simeon), published in 1879.

Bertinoro, Obadiah of. 1450—1510. Rabbinical scholar and Mishnaic commentator, born in Bertinoro, northern Italy. Extract from his letters published under the title *Ha-Masa le-Eretz Yisrael* (Journey to the Land of Israel).

Byron. Lord. 1788—1824. Famous English poet, born in London. Extract from *Hebrew Melodies.*

Chateaubriand, François René. 1768—1848. Prominent French statesman and writer. Visited the Land of Israel in 1806—1807. Extract from his book on the Land of Israel, published in Paris in 1811.

De Linne, Charles Josef. 1735—1804. Belgian prince and general. Extract from his memorandum on the Jews, 1797.

Disraeli, Benjamin (Earl of Beaconsfield). 1804—1881. British statesman and novelist. Visited the Land of Israel in 1831. Extract from his book *Alroy.*

Dumas, Alexandre, fils. 1824—1895. Well known French writer. Extract from his play *La Femme de Claude.*

Duran, Simeon son of Zemah. 1361—1444. Rabbi, philosopher and physician, who lived in Algiers from 1391.

Emden, Jacob. 1698—1776. Talmudist and author, who lived in Altona, Germany. Extract from the introduction to his Commentary on the Prayer Book.

Farhi, Isaac. ?—1853. Rabbi, writer of religious literature, emissary from Israel to Jewish communities in Europe. Extract from his composition *Mituv Haaretz.*

Flavius, Josephus. c. 38—100 C.E. Jewish military leader and historian at the time of the Jewish revolt against the Romans in the first century.

Hasselkvist, Friedrich. 18th century. From Sweden, doctor. Extract from his book, printed in Stockholm, 1757.

Helo, Isaac. 18th century. From his book *Shviley Yerushalaim* (The Pats of Jerusalem).

Hurwitz, Isaiah ha-Levy. 1570—c.1630. Rabbi and Cabbalist, known as "Shilo Hakadosh". Dayan and head of Yeshivah in Prague, came to Israel in 1621. Extract from *Shevet Yehuda.*

Itinerarium Burdigalense. Written by a pilgrim from Bordeaux who apparently visited Jerusalem in 333 C.E. The extract from his travel book was first published in 1898 in Vienna, in a collection of travel descriptions by P. Geyer.

Jerome. 342—420. Latin Church Father. Extract from his commentary on Zephaniah 1:15, written in 392.

Jessie, Henry. 17th century. English Christian priest. Extract from his pamphlet *An Information Concerning the Present State of the Jewish Nation in Europe and Judea, etc.,* published in London, 1658.

Judah ha-Levi. 1075—1141. Religious philosopher, and the greatest Hebrew poet of the Middle Ages.

Kabatnik, Martin. Monk from Bohemia, who visited the Land of Israel in 1491—1492.

Kerr, Alfred. 1867—1948. German literary critic and author, who visited the Land of Israel in 1903.

Latif, Isaac. Rabbi, who came from Italy to Israel at the end of the 15th century. Extract from letter he sent to Italy.

Levinski, Elchanan Leib. 1857—1910. Russo-Jewish writer. Extract from his book on the Land of Israel, published in 1890.

Maimonides (Moses son of Maimon). 1135—1205. The greatest medieval Jewish scholar. Rabbi, legalist, commentator, philosopher and physician, born in Cordova, Spain.

Marx, Karl. 1818—1883. Philosopher of modern socialism. Extract from essay in New York Daily Tribune, 15.4.1854.

*Mohilever, Samuel.*1824—1898. One of the greatest Rabbis in Russia, active Zionist, among the leaders of the early Russian Zionist movement "Hovivey Zion". Extract from essay.

Nahmanides (Moses son of Nahman). c. 1194–1270. One of the greatest of Jewish sages, legalist, biblical commentator and liturgical poet, born in Gerona, Spain, who came to the Land of Israel at the age of seventy-three. Extract from letter to his son, which is published in its entirety at the end of his commentary on the Pentateuch.

Rashi (Solomon son of Isaac). 1040–1105. Most famous of all biblical and Talmudic commentators. Lived in the Rhineland.

Sahal son of Mazliah. Karaite sage of the 10th century, and author of commentaries on the Psalms and Ecclesiastes. Extract from the introduction to his Book of Commandments.

Salman son of Yeruham. Karaite sage of the 10th century, who was born in Egypt and active in Jerusalem 940–960.

Skili, Jacob. 14th century. Rabbi, born in Sicily, Italy.

Solomon, Joel Moses. 1838–1912. Writer and journalist, among the founders of the settlement Petah-Tikva, 1878 (today a city in Israel). Extract from his recitations on settling in Israel.

Tudela, Benjamin of. Rabbi, embarked on voyages in 1165 and returned to his country after 8 years. Extract from his book *Mas'ot Binyamin.*

Volterra, Meshullam of. Rabbi from Italy, who came to Israel in 1481.

Yerushalmi, Moses. Extract from the book *Mas'ot R. Moshe Yerushalmi* (Itineraries), 1769.

Zimpel, Dr. Charles Franz. 1801–?. German philosopher, doctor and naturalist, who came to Jerusalem in 1852. Extract from his booklet on the Israelis in Jerusalem.

Classical Jewish sources which contain legal writings, pronouncements and dicta of the Jewish sages throughout the centuries. Quotations have been included from the:

Talmudim (Babylonian and Jerusalem): Tractates Berakhoth, Sukkah, Hagigah, Ketuboth, Kiddushin, Baba Bathra.

Toseftha: Tractates Sukkah, Sotah.

Midrashim: Midrash Rabbah, Pirke de-Rabbi Eliezer, Shoher Tov, Pesikta Rabbati, Tanhuma, Yalkut Shimeoni.

The English versions of the biblical texts
are taken from "The Holy Scriptures,"
published by the Jewish Publication Society of America.